CURSIVE HANDWRITING WORKBOOK GRADE 3
Children's Reading & Writing Education Books

SPEEDY PUBLISHING

Speedy Publishing LLC
40 E. Main St. #1156
Newark, DE 19711
www.speedypublishing.com

Copyright 2016

All Rights reserved. No part of this book may be reproduced or used in any way or form or by any means whether electronic or mechanical, this means that you cannot record or photocopy any material ideas or tips that are provided in this book

Trace the letters.
Say the name and
sound of the letter.

Aa Aa

A a

A A A A A a a a a a

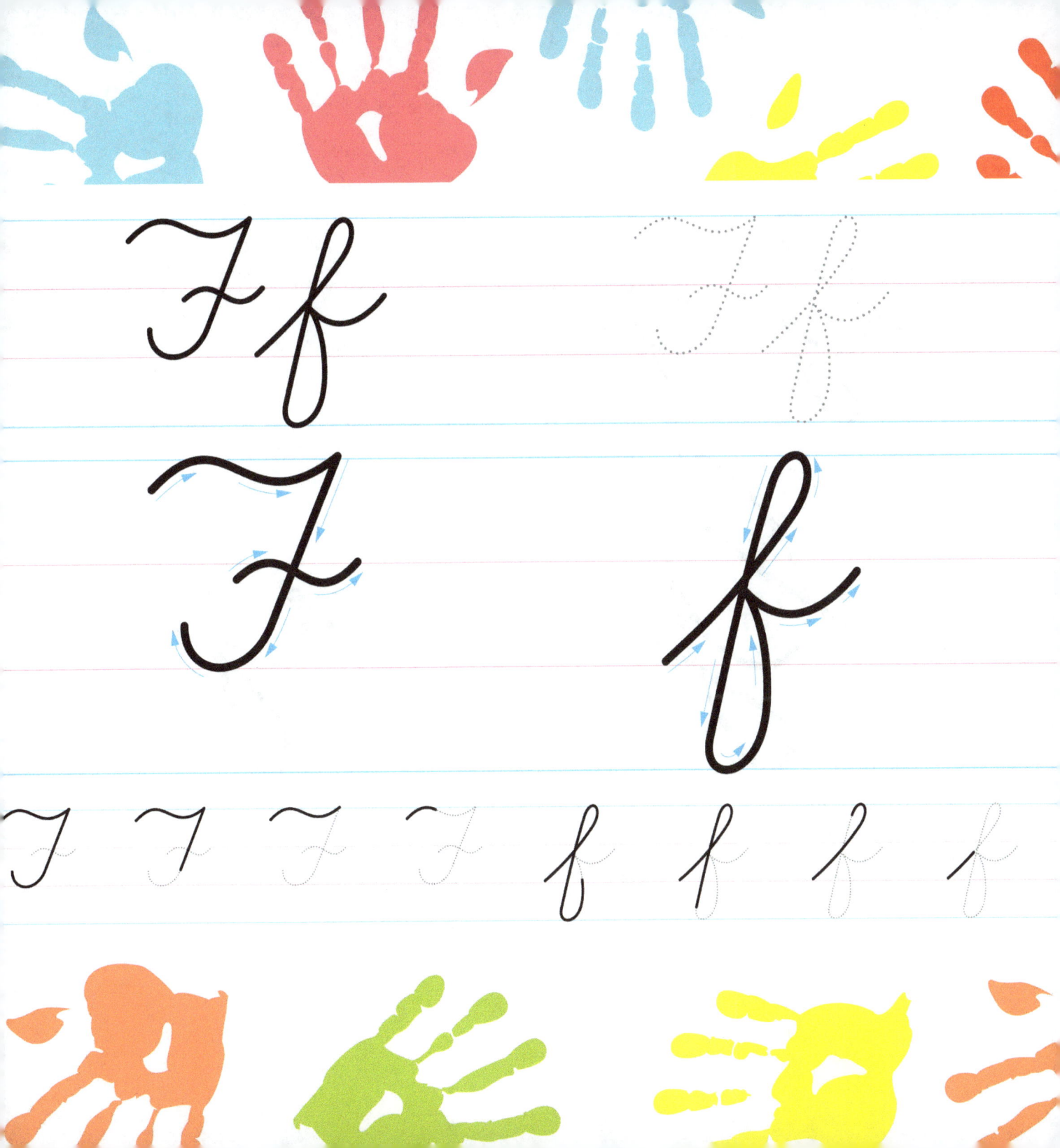

𝒢 𝑔

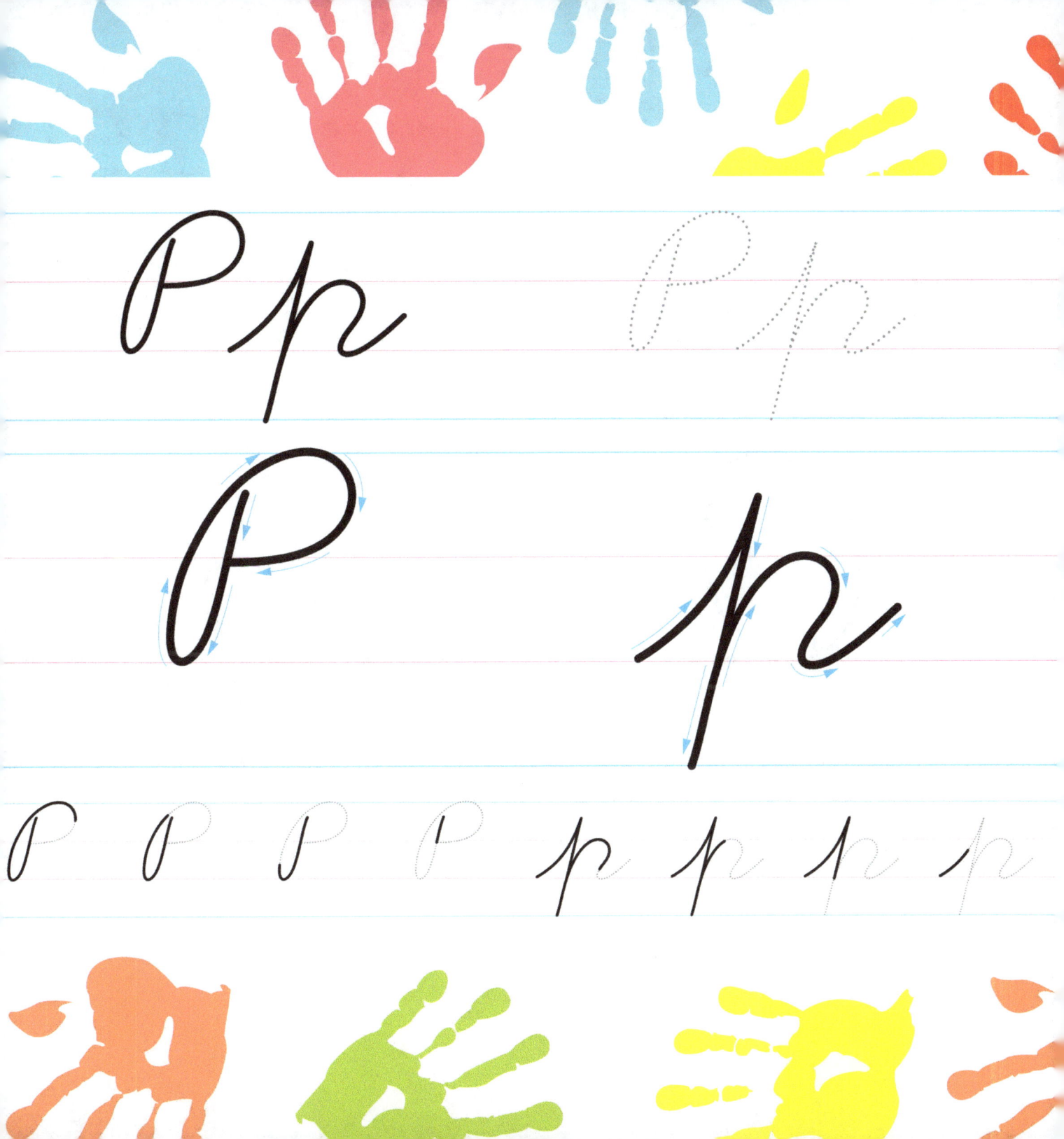

Tt

И и

Y y

Trace the words.

Say the words.

every

school

keep

beauty

decimal

element

atom

graph

lady

close

object

east

dog

tiger

monkey

giraffe

happy

lesson

word

win

street

story

near

water

phone

gadget

chair

paper

table

grow

light

hole

write

drink

grow

toys

www.ingramcontent.com/pod-product-compliance
Lightning Source LLC
LaVergne TN
LVHW061322060426
835507LV00019B/2259